Shor

Use These Super-Fast and Easy Ways to Get Instant Cash!

By: Edward Clark

9781635012613

PUBLISHERS NOTES

Disclaimer – Speedy Publishing LLC

This publication is intended to provide helpful and informative material. It is not intended to diagnose, treat, cure, or prevent any health problem or condition, nor is intended to replace the advice of a physician. No action should be taken solely on the contents of this book. Always consult your physician or qualified health-care professional on any matters regarding your health and before adopting any suggestions in this book or drawing inferences from it.

The author and publisher specifically disclaim all responsibility for any liability, loss or risk, personal or otherwise, which is incurred as a consequence, directly or indirectly, from the use or application of any contents of this book.

Any and all product names referenced within this book are the trademarks of their respective owners. None of these owners have sponsored, authorized, endorsed, or approved this book.

Always read all information provided by the manufacturers' product labels before using their products. The author and publisher are not responsible for claims made by manufacturers.

This book was originally printed before 2014. This is an adapted reprint by Speedy Publishing LLC with newly updated content designed to help readers with much more accurate and timely information and data.

Speedy Publishing LLC

40 E Main Street, Newark, Delaware, 19711

Contact Us: 1-888-248-4521

Website: http://www.speedypublishing.co

REPRINTED Paperback Edition: 9781635012613:

Manufactured in the United States of America

Dedication

This book is dedicated to Louise. I will forever be your "Clark".

Table of Contents

Chapter 1- Why Everyone Dreams of but Only a Few Achieves Instant Money 5

Chapter 2- The Two Categories of Online Marketing 10

Chapter 3- Selling Skills and Services from the Other End of the World 16

Chapter 4- Hooking Up with the Largest Money-Making Machines Online 21

Chapter 5- The Emerging Popularity and Value of PLR 25

Chapter 6- Write or Teach for Your Love of Money 39

Chapter 7- You Have Potential Income with Affiliate Marketing 47

Chapter 8- Domain Flipping and Website Spinning 49

About The Author 62

Chapter 1 - Why Everyone Dreams of but Only a Few Achieves Instant Money

There are thousands of websites and eBooks that tell you can earn thousands of dollars a day by working online, if you will only buy their eBooks with the magic formula for just 49.99 dollars or so! How much of this is true? There are a lot of scams which spout some lame gibberish once they have relieved you of some hard earned money. Those who fall for such tricks only have themselves to blame. There no shortcuts to riches online. It's just like real life, where you work hard and sensibly and earn your daily bread.

Just as in real life, you have to use the skills that you have and also keep acquiring new ones. Just as in a real-time job, you have to work a certain number of hours a day to earn your online living.

Short on Cash?

And just as in real life, only those workers who study their job well, steer clear of fraudsters and work hard and skillfully will do well and earn a sizeable income online.

The next chapters will take a hard look at the various ways you can earn money online for every hour of work that you put in. There are millions of people all over the world who are already working on these online jobs from the comfort of their homes. You can be your own boss, decide how many hours you want to work and get paid through international systems like PayPal or even by check in your own local currency.

Remember, today's world is a socially networked world. The Net has put a lot of knowledge at your fingertips. Even if you feel you don't have formal degrees and training, if you have the will, you can learn fast. You can use your grasp of English, your ability to use the Internet and your social circle of friends to develop your skills. And then you can quickly start earning on at least some of the areas discussed ahead.

Breaking Down the Concept of Easy and Instant Cash

The global market is extremely volatile. We get news from the media all day wondering if we will be facing the next economic meltdown weeks from now.

Investments and traditional businesses are no longer the pot of gold at the end of the rainbow. People feel that any investment that requires cash up front is usually met with skepticism as more and more businesses fail within the first 2 years of operation.

Another reason why people need fast cash strategies is because the majority of 'business opportunities' out there require a monetary investment.

Industries like network marketing or Forex or investments all require some money in order to start a business. Although these industries are HIGHLY profitable, many people are not willing to fork out cash to get a business started.

The only business that is completely cost-free is Internet marketing. Please note that there are certain business models that:

    Require money

    Do not require money or less than $100

We will only talk about models that require less than $100. All you need is your own personal effort – trading your time for money, that's all.

No money up front, no interviews and no risk. Just your time, that's all.

I call these business models – NO COST, FAST PROFIT.

Unlike what people say in buy low, sell high, I'm not even going to get you to invest any money and you do not need to wait weeks or months to get the money. A few days (and sometimes, in extreme cases... a few hours) is all that is needed to get the money rolling.

These business models are also considered an 'Iron Rice Bowl'. (This is a Chinese term that means a business or career path that is immune to retrenchment or failure)

All you need to do is to get started implementing these strategies because the only way you can fail is to read about it and do nothing.

Short on Cash?
How it Works

Let's talk about how we can get instant fast cash.

The key is to leverage on other people's resources:

> Leveraging on their massive traffic

> Existing buyer's needs

> Free Search Engine traffic like Google

> Or even selling free stuff for good price (high value involved)

There are a few ways you can look for fast cash. You can make money through affiliate marketing or AdSense, but you must have traffic to come to your site. Since buying traffic is not really an option, your best bet is to leverage on Web 2.0 sites, article directories, press releases, blogs or forums to get those visitors to come to your website.

There are many degrees of buyers as well. There are people who are already pre-sold on the value of the product and there are others who are not in that category.

The goal is to go for these types of 'low-hanging fruit' because they are the easiest customers to 'close'. In fact, they are probably ready to buy with credit card (or PayPal account ready) in hand; it is just a matter of whether you are the affiliate credited for the sale or if it goes to someone else.

So you might as well be the one to cash in.

Google is also a very good place to get traffic. Using Social Bookmarking, you shouldn't have a problem getting ranked on lower competitive keywords – for example, if you write a review on Squidoo or Hub Pages, you can leverage on their 'rank authority' and get listed on Google.

Lastly, there are many products with Master Resell Rights of Private Label Rights available on the Internet.

There are many places where you can easily and quickly obtain a large collection of products with Master Resell Rights or Private Label Rights. All you need to do is to look for these products on popular Internet marketing blogs or newsletters by subscribing to them.

You can easily make use of these products (they can be obtained at a relatively cheap price) and you can sell them off for a hefty profit (the following chapters will reveal how).

All you have to remember is this – you have all the resources you will ever need to produce fast cash, so do not worry about a lack of resources.

Chapter 2- The Two Categories of Online Marketing

In online marketing terms, these services could probably be allocated to two different categories.

Specialized Skills

Specialized services are those that require a degree of technical skill or ability. If you have any experience in any specialized area such as creating websites, software programming or writing copy for sales pages, you already have everything you need to start making money on the net pretty much straight away. What you need to do is bring your abilities to the notice of your customer base.

The benefit of providing specialized services is because it is not something everyone can do; you can charge premium prices for your services.

For example, a top sales page copywriter is able to command a five-figure sum for just one sales page.

If you're not in the position to if not, there is no reason why you cannot train yourself to acquire the necessary skills. Many of these skills can be learned over a period of time because everything you need to know is available on the net for free.

For example, if you want to learn how to create highly professional HTML web pages, there are many online tutorials where you can learn HTML from the ground up.

Creating software programs is an excellent way of generating a very healthy income and it is not hard to learn. Furthermore there is always a demand for software programs. Once again, if you search the net for information about how to create software, there are free teaching materials available, so you can learn even if you have no experience of writing software or creating scripts whatsoever.

Of course, if providing some form of specialized service is something that is of interest to you, it is not something that you will be able to do straight away with no previous experience.

If you're not yet ready to offer specialized services, you can subsidize your activities with non-specialized services.

Non-Specialized Services

This category includes services such as writing, creating graphic images (i.e. drawing, painting or photographing images that you sell) and other web specific services such as link building. Most people can offer these services without needing extensive training.

Short on Cash?

For instance, even if you haven't written anything apart from a shopping list since you left high school, more than likely, all you need is a bit of practice to get you back into the swing of it.

This is worth considering because there is a huge demand on the net for written content (for web pages, article publication and so on). As a result, anyone who can write a half-decent article can make money doing so.

Website owners need a constant supply of material for their online marketing activities. At a rate of $5-10 per article, you can easily earn a $100 or more per day.

Where to Look for Clients

Once you've decided to offer your services, the most important thing to know is where to find clients; because you can be certain they won't come looking for you.

For a newcomer the easiest place to offer your services are on forums where you'll be dealing directly with the client - Such as through the 'Services' forum page at Digital Point which is a well-known online marketing forum site. On this site, there are several different categories of service which you can provide, all you need to do is decide upon is the appropriate category for the service that you are going to provide.

For example, there are many people who use this site who will pay others to post on forums or blogs on their behalf:

Okay, this is not going to make your fortune, but as the average forum posting is going to be somewhere between 25 and 100 words, it is not a great deal of work either.

And of course, you could extend this concept to a point where you can start to generate a reasonable amount of income from something as simple as making forum or blog postings:

For example, if you were going to write articles or reports for other online marketers, then you would list your services under the 'Content Creation' sub-category.

Another leading forum site where you can offer your services directly to end-users is the Warrior Forum, arguably the number one online marketing forum.

This site has a sub-forum known as the Warrior Special Offers (WSO) section where for $20; you can post any special offer that you want to make available to other Warrior members, with the only proviso being that the 'deal' has to be something that is not available elsewhere:

So for example, if you are offering to write 500 word article is for $7 elsewhere, you might offer to do the same for Warrior members for $5 because as long as the offer is an exclusive and it provides value to other members, it will be accepted.

That $20 will put your offer in front of hundreds of potential customers, all of whom will at some point need the services that you provide. Even if it is your very first time of offering your services, I can almost guarantee that you will get some takers. In addition, the Warrior forum has a section called Warrior for Hire, which costs $20 as well but is more appropriate for long-term exposure and advertising.

Alternatively there are the freelance sites such as Elance, Get a Freelancer, vWorkers (Formerly RentACoder), Script Lance and Guru.com. You can register your services with all of the sites free

Short on Cash?

and as they are sites to which every webmaster goes to find freelance workers for specific projects, they are great sites through which to find work.

As you will see if you look at the different sites, some of them specialize in programmers and coders, whereas sites like Elance and Get a Freelancer are less specifically targeted. Nevertheless, it still makes sense to register your services with all of them, as net entrepreneurs will regularly look at all of them when they are looking to someone who can do a specific job.

Webmasters also list their jobs as well, so you can 'pitch' for work as well as uploading your details to the site.

The competition is fierce on these freelance sites and without a proven record of accomplishment; it may be rather difficult to land that first job.

You therefore have to give some thought to how you can attract your first clients. One option is of course to charge less but don't go too low.

The advantage of using forums such as Digital Point and the Warrior forum is that you are dealing with Webmasters and other online entrepreneurs directly. It is a one-to-one service with no intermediary (as there is when you use one of the freelance sites) which means that things can often be organized more quickly and easily.

On the other hand, using a freelance site as an 'intermediary' does have some advantages. The site will for example handle payments in a 100% safe manner whereas if you are dealing directly with your customer, you have to handle this yourself.

Nevertheless, going through a forum site like Digital Point does enable you to find customers quickly and easily, and you should of course ask your satisfied customers for testimonials and endorsements after you have finished every job.

Chapter 3 - Selling Skills and Services from the Other End of the World

One of the fastest ways you can make fast money is by selling skills and services.

Can you do the following?

- Write articles

- Create beautiful graphics

- Debug or install a software or script

- Speak with an audible voice

- Even something as simple as submitting articles to article directories or comment on other people's blogs

Let me tell you this – you can easily trade your skills for big money, especially if you are staying outside the U.S. and the currency conversion rate works to your favor. (Yes, even submitting articles for people or doing simple SEO work can be a very good way to get fast cash).

I've personally made tens of thousands of dollars just by providing writing services to people and it has single handedly funded my Internet marketing business while I was building it up. Today, I do not write as much but I outsource a lot of writing to other people thanks to my established Internet marketing business.

All you need to do is go to where the clients are!

The first thing you must do is to create your own account or sign up as a member on outsourcing sites. You will need these accounts to apply for projects there.

By going to those sites will teach you how to create your own account there. You can post or bids for jobs while you are there.

Bear in mind, when you are just starting out, nobody knows who you are so you will have to earn people's trust. The fastest way to get noticed is to show good samples of what you are capable of and bid really, really low. You will get offers or opportunities if they see value in your work.

Make sure you bid for as many projects as you can. The biggest pitfall would be to bid for 2 or 3 projects and sit there and wait. If you are really desperate for money, make sure you bid for every single project you are capable of (if you can handle all of them).

Now, someone may ask...

Short on Cash?
"What if I have none of the skills and services listed above?"

Good question!

As a matter of fact, you can bid more jobs than you can handle and OUTSOURCE these jobs to other freelancers!

In other words, you the MIDDLE-man by bidding for projects and outsourcing to others even if you are not good at the skill or you are not willing to spend time working on it.

You can either outsource to other freelancing agents, or to people that you may know around your location. Preferably, it is better to go for someone you trust. The key to getting projects done is to consistently bid and outsource to the same person without telling them where you get the job (that way you can keep your profit margins higher.)

How to Boost Your Website's Traffic and Earn Money

I will share with you 4 strategies to get fast traffic to your website and make money via affiliate marketing or AdSense:

1.   Social Bookmarking

Social Bookmarking is one of the easiest ways to get fast and instant traffic to your website. This strategy is quite viable because there are millions of visitors visiting those pages on a daily basis. Sometimes, they even send out newsletters to recycle the traffic. Either way, it is one of the easiest ways to get people to come to your site.

2. Article Directory Submission

Writing articles and submitting them to directories is a very easy way to get targeted traffic and increase your search engine rankings.

You can write a review and place your affiliate link on a Squidoo or Hub Page and drive traffic using a combination of Social Bookmarking and article directory submission. As long as you use a proper anchor text for your keyword you will be able to rank for certain terms easily.

A good example of using anchor text is to link a keyword like "Fat Loss 4 Idiots" rather than http://www.fatloss4idiots.com in the author bio box.

3. Submit Press Releases

A press release is like a news center where it publishes the latest news.

4. Comment on Other People's Blogs

One of the easiest ways to get fast traffic is to comment on other people's blogs.

Of course, you must make sure you do the following:

-   Choose high traffic blogs (e.g. John Chow, ShoeMoney, ProBlogger, etc.)

-   Make sure you are one of the first few people to post the comment there.

Short on Cash?
Bear in mind, never, ever spam your comments. Don't write one liners like "Good Post", or "Nice Blog"... make sure you post something constructive.

CHAPTER 4- HOOKING UP WITH THE LARGEST MONEY-MAKING MACHINES ONLINE

One of the most popular advertising programs on the Internet is Google's AdSense. Almost any website you open today has those 'Ads by Google' placed at the left or right or bottom of the page. Sometimes they are even bang in the center. Every time you click on such an ad, that webmaster is paid a small amount by the advertiser, through Google's AdSense. Every day millions of dollars are being paid out on AdSense clicks through billions of page views. This makes Google's AdSense the most popular Pay per Click (PPC) program in the world today.

Short on Cash?

The payment per click can range from a few cents to even ten or twenty dollars. Niche content relevant to certain specialized keywords can pay very highly. But merely setting up a website with these high paying keywords and placing AdSense ads on it isn't going to work. The site has to contain information that is valuable to the reader. Only then will it generate enough traffic and genuine ad clicks. If you click on your own ads or ask your friends to deliberately click to benefit you, AdSense admin will knock off the ads from your webpage faster than you can say 'click fraud'!

So it is wise to set up a website or blog based on a subject you like, which is also commercially viable – there have to be some advertisers who would like to place their ads on your pages. AdSense bots will scan your webpages every day and then place ads relevant to your content.

You can use blogger.com to set up a simple blog in three easy steps. Then read up on your subject and write original content. Make sure you mention the keywords relevant to your content. Then generate traffic to your website by emailing your blog link to your friends and ask them to pass it on. Place the link on your friends' websites too and also take part in forums connected to your topic.

Use a traffic monitoring website like Sitemeter.com to check on how much page views and hits you get every day. Your AdSense account page will also tell you how many clicks have been made and how much you have earned. You can receive your payment by various methods as explained on your account page. AdSense also has good advice on how to place the ads for maximum profitability.

So get started with your blog or website and power it up with Google AdSense!

Edward Clark
Spend Your Spare Hours at the Mechanical Turk

Ever wondered how you could make some extra dollars in your spare hours? Mechanical Turk offers you just that.

This website is owned by Amazon, the online marketing giant. Mturk.com displays thousands of HITs (Human Intelligence Tasks) on its pages. These tasks range from simple to complex and the payment for doing them also ranges from a few cents up to even tens of dollars. The simpler tasks can involve taking a survey or writing a few paragraphs on a given subject or commenting on a particular forum. The more complex ones can require some web design or writing entire reports or doing some market research. There are also audio transcription jobs that can fetch you a few dollars for transcribing 5-10 minutes long audio clips into text.

Mturk is a great way to train up for more specialized online jobs. If you start writing a few 100 or 200 word articles here, you can gain the skills and confidence to take up larger freelance writing assignments on sites like ODesk, Elance and GetAFreelancer, which we will discuss in the next chapters.

If you get the hang of audio transcription and become reasonably accurate and fast enough, you can eventually move on to fulltime medical or legal transcriptions which are high paying fields. You have to train up for these specialized areas, but Mechanical Turk gives you a good start with simple tasks.

Within a few hours or days, your work is checked and payment is credited to your Mturk account. The trick is to be on the lookout for high paying tasks, where for example you earn a couple of dollars for a survey which takes only a few minutes. Or writing a 400 word article on Tourism in Iceland which earns you 3 dollars! Even if you are not familiar with the topic, you can quickly read up

Short on Cash?

on the Net and make a fairly decent and factual presentation. After all that's what many journalists and media writers are doing today!

Payments are made by checks in local currency (for certain countries) or transferred to your bank account, or you can use the money in your account to purchase goods from Amazon.com.

A good way to get started on thousands of easy tasks and train up for bigger things to come! Don't let a spare hour go to waste. Become a Turker today. And don't forget to browse a good Turker forum for the latest buzz and loads of good and useful advice.

Chapter 5 - The Emerging Popularity and Value of PLR

When it comes to making money online, there are short-cut strategies available that will maximize your income, and minimize the time and effort you spend developing your online business.

As you know, in order to make money in your chosen niche, you need to be able to offer your own info product. Not only is this a guaranteed method of generating passive, recurring income from a product you develop once, but it also allows you to penetrate your niche market in a different way, by building a targeted mailing list of relevant leads.

The problem comes into play when you don't have the money, time or resources to develop your own product.

Short on Cash?

Not only can creating an info product be exceptionally time consuming, but if you don't have the necessary skills in order to write the content yourself, you may find it very expensive to outsource the work to an experienced freelance writer.

But there's an even better, cheaper and faster method of developing high quality content that is guaranteed to be gobbled up by prospects within your market.

Best of all, by tapping into this wealth of information and resources, you can maximize your outreach by diving into dozens of niche markets without ever having to be an expert on the subject. In fact, you can use this secret weapon to power up as many websites as you wish, without ever having to type a line of text yourself, or deal with costly freelancers.

It's called private label, and is often referred to online as PLR, which stands for 'private label rights'.

With PLR, you are able to take someone else's work and transform it into your very own customized product, where you can brand it as your own, attach your name to the material and even modify, edit or remove any content that is unwanted.

You can also sell this content based on your own price structure, and will be able to claim 100% of all profits generated from sales, without having to share in the commissions, wait for payment from affiliate programs, or pay royalties to the original developer.

But using standard private label won't give you the cutting edge over your competition. In fact, if you want to stand out from the crowd, and generate as much attention, revenue and traffic to your website by powering it up with fresh private label content, you need to take things to a whole new level.

I will show you exactly how I personally use private label content to build a complete powerhouse of profitable websites, all designed to funnel in hungry buyers, and consistently build massive mailing lists of targeted leads.

By using private label resources, not only will you be able to instantly begin building a solid platform of high profit websites, but you will spend LESS time, while making MORE money than other marketers who are spending countless hours creating their own info products, or pouring thousands of dollars into development costs for projects that they aren't even sure will pan out.

Private label is not only an effective method of generating consistent income from the sales of the products themselves, but you can use it to quickly test out markets and evaluate the profitability before spending the time and money creating your very own custom product.

I will reveal the powerful strategies I've used over the years to quickly monetize private label, while adding thousands of dollars to my backend with additional quick-cash tactics that will further maximize your results.

It's an exciting opportunity to take existing products and exploit countless niche markets, quickly and easily.

Do You Lose Your Rights with PLRs?

It's important that you thoroughly read through this chapter before you ever decide to use private label, so that you fully understand the terminology as well as the exact rights and restrictions often associated with various licenses and releases.

Short on Cash?

To start, there are three different licenses common in the PLR industry:

Resell Rights (RR)

With Resell Rights, permission is granted by the product owner that allows you to simply resell the product. You are not permitted to modify the content, edit the content or add additional material to the content, in fact, you are rarely provided with the source (doc) file to be able to edit anything at all.

With resell rights, you cannot pass on any rights to your customers, meaning that they will purchase only personal rights to the product with no additional rights.

Resell rights are always subject to various terms and conditions provided by the product developer, and can go so far as to how you are able to market the product, or distribute the product.

With so many restrictions in place, it's often difficult to use resell rights products to further your own brand, as it's quite common that the original developer will incorporate their name and website URL within the product itself.

What does this mean?

You will end up spending time and resources promoting someone else's brand, rather than your own.

When it comes to making money online with your own product line, you'll want to avoid products that only offer resell rights, unless you intend to feature them only as added upsells or bonus products.

Master Resell Rights (MRR)

With MRR, Master Resell Rights, you are usually allowed to both sell the product with personal rights to your customers, or sell the rights as well, so that your customer can also sell the product to their customer.

Generally, products featuring MRR will cost more per license than those with RR due to the added flexibility offered with these types of releases.

Private Label Rights (PLR)

With PLR, Private Label Rights, you are given the most flexibility of all, including being able to modify the document or content, add your name as the signature author, and sell and distribute the product however you wish.

When purchasing any kind of license rights, you want to request clear documentation outlining your rights, so that in the event you are ever questioned about your authority to use or repurpose the content, you can provide a license created by the original developer outlining your options and permissions.

If you ever purchase a PLR or a MRR package that does not include a copy of your rights, then do NOT use it in any way until you contact the developer directly and request a copy of the terms associated with the package. You always need to protect yourself from future claims or problems.

When it comes to making the most money online using pre-created content, you will want to primarily focus on PLR (Private Label) rather than MRR or RR.

Short on Cash?

The reason is a simple one, with PLR you can focus on building your own brand, credibility and reputation within your niche market by using the products and material as if it were originally developed by you or your company.

To do this, you will want to spend a few minutes tweaking each package that you intend to use.

Assuming that the PLR content that you pick is likely to be unrestricted, the limit on what you can do with them is really down to your own imagination and abilities.

As one example, it is very common to pick up PLR e-book's which you can use in a wide variety of ways.

One option is to take the book that you have just obtained before republishing it as-is, without making any alterations at all. This approach is generally not going to be particularly viable however, because whilst in theory you can add your own name to the book as the writer and republish it immediately, the chances are that other people have already done exactly the same thing (probably many times over).

Hence, what you are republishing is duplicate content, a book that is exactly the same as the one that has been published by one or 10 or even 100 other online entrepreneurs. Furthermore, you have added no additional value to the PLR pack, so what is the main selling point of your product?

This is definitely something that you do not want to do as it is a guaranteed way of acquiring dissatisfied (refund seeking) customers and represents a very quick way of destroying your reputation as well.

On the other hand, there is nothing whatsoever to stop you rewriting significant chunks of the book before republishing it as your own work, but this is just one option. Alternatively, you might break up the text into articles, short reports, blog or website content, e-zine articles, e-mail messages or basically whatever else you can think of.

In addition, there are many sites where you can find PLR article materials in which case, you can to an extent reverse the process by bringing these article materials together into a short report or an e-book.

Optionally, you might rewrite these articles so that they become unique (it should take no more than 20 minutes per piece) before submitting your work to the article directory sites.

Submitting articles to directories like these is a superb way of driving targeted visitors to your business enabled website, a tactic which thousands of marketers do every day with a great deal of success.

However, you should always check that your article is unique before submitting by running it through Copyscape and it is also necessary to make sure that you submit to EzineArticles and wait for them to publish your work before submitting elsewhere. This is because they insist on publishing only unique work and because a human editor will review your submitted work; it generally takes two or three days before they publish.

Other types of PLR content materials that are becoming more widely available are audios and videos, although the vast majority of PLR content still tends to be written materials.

Short on Cash?

Let's take a quick look at the different PLR sources available online that provide consistent updates and fresh releases covering a wide variety of niche markets.

One obvious example was highlighted in the previous chapter as many content writers offer PLR materials through Warrior Special Offers. Hence, you can use the forum as a buyer of valuable content rather than as a seller as well.

Beyond this, there are plenty of websites where you can buy PLR materials and quite a few places where you can get such content for free.

As a general rule, I am a big fan of using free materials and resources whenever possible, but when it comes to PLR content around which you are going to build your business; it often makes more sense to spend a little money than it does to use free materials.

This is because of the scarcity factor highlighted in the previous chapter. It is a fact that the more scarce the content you are using is, the more value it has.

This is one reason why many paid PLR content sites have a limit on the number of new members they accept as by imposing this limit, they ensure that the content materials are not owned by every Tom, Dick and Harry who uses the net.

The problem here is, the more people that own a particular PLR e-book or special report, the harder it is for you to create unique content materials from that source.

Hence, it takes a great deal of time to turn those materials into something valuable that you have a realistic chance of selling. In effect, it is a question of balancing the value of your time against money because if you use free PLR materials, it is going to take you considerably longer to create something that is unique than it would if you paid for those materials from a restricted members site.

Okay, so let's say that you have bought a niche targeted PLR e-book and that you want to start making money from it as quickly as possible.

How do you do this?

The quickest and easiest way of using your PLR product to start generating an income is to create a simple website to sell the book from. Make sure that enough of the book is rewritten for the final version to be unique and then start selling it for $17 or $27 per copy.

In order to do so, the first thing that you need is a list of keyword terms related to the niche market on which your book is focused.

These are the words or phrases that people use when they search the net for information of the kind that is featured in your book. Keywords are extremely important because they are literally the key to the success of your business.

Say that you have got an e-book that is focused on the 'weight loss' market, which is an incredibly popular net search.

What you need to establish is what words or phrases people use to search for weight loss related information and in order to do this, there are a couple of free tools that you should use.

Short on Cash?

The first tool is the free Word Tracker keyword research tool with which you can find the 100 most regularly searched phrases in your market niche.

According to Word Tracker, there are in excess of 40,000 Google searches every day for weight loss information, with the most popular search term being 'weight loss' itself. However, this not a phrase that you can use in your own marketing efforts because of the competition levels indicated by a Google search:

There are nearly 66,000,000 results listed by Google for this particular term, which is far too many for you to stand a realistic chance of achieving a decent search results page position.

However, by running a similar competition search for each term that Word Tracker produces, you should be able to find weight loss related phrases where the competition levels are reasonable. You are ideally looking for 30,000 (or less) competing results when you run an exact match search (i.e. your search term in "inverted commas").

Move down the Word Tracker table and you will find many keyword terms of this type. However, the disadvantage of using the free version of Word Tracker is that it only produces the top 100 keyword phrases for your market, which might mean that you only find two or three keyword terms that you can use after running your competition checks.

Consequently, the other free tool that you should look to build a more comprehensive list of keyword phrases which you use in your marketing efforts is Google's own free keyword research tool.

With your keyword list in place, the next thing is to register a domain name from which you can sell your new book. If possible, you should register a domain name that uses one of your primary keyword phrases as this is one of the most effective ways of making sure that the search engines find your site for the keyword which you are targeting.

There are plenty of sites where you can register a new domain name but amongst the online marketing community. As every domain on the net is completely unique, you will probably find that the most popular keyword phrases that you might target as a domain name will already have been taken. Consequently, you might need to add dashes between the different words in order to grab a domain name which is appropriate to your site.

You will note that at the time of writing, the .info domain name is incredibly cheap which if money is an issue might make it appealing to use this particular form of domain name. However, if you can afford to buy the .com version, it is generally more effective to do so and more professional as well, primarily because most searchers still think of the internet as the dot-com world.

Okay, with your domain name registered, you need to set up a hosting account, with the $7.95 HostGator 'Baby' shared account option being a firm favorite for online marketers.

The final thing that you need to do is to tie your domain name together with your host which you do by following the instructions for 'Changing the nameservers' that you will find approximately 2/3 of the way down this HostGator support page:

Next, you need to create a simple website from which to sell your product. Keep this as simple as possible, with one option being to search Google for (before downloading and installing) a free sales page template.

Short on Cash?
Alternatively, you could install and use WordPress with free sales-optimized 'themes' (templates) being available on all these sites at the time of writing.

Install your new sales template or theme to your site and add a thank you page from where anyone who buys your product can download it. Add your PayPal 'Buy Now' button to your main page and link that button to the download page on your site so that anyone who buys will be immediately redirected to the download by PayPal.

Okay, you are now ready to start selling, which means sending targeted visitors to your site as quickly as possible.

There are several ways that you do this, all of which are focused on using your keyword terms in promotional materials that you publish on external sites.

The first thing you can do is create a very short video that you post to YouTube. Find two or three useless facts or bits of trivia that are somehow related to your niche, and create three questions based on those facts.

Next, type the simplest question into the first slide of a PowerPoint or an Open Office presentation. On the next slide, add the answer, with the third slide being the next question followed by the answer and so on. Leave a few seconds between each slide in your video to give the viewer time to think (i.e. get them 'involved').

However, the answer to the third and most difficult question should not be included in this video but instead, post it on your site. After 'pulling in' anyone who sees this video with the first two questions and answers, you then send them to your site to get the final answer by including the URL and a specific instruction telling them to visit your site in the last slide of your presentation.

Use free screen capture software like CamStudio to make the video and don't forget to include a couple of your major keyword terms in both the title of your video and your description. However, make sure that the first line of your description is the URL of your site (including the 'http://www' bit at the beginning) as doing this ensures that you add a clickable link from your video to your site.

Next, find the most popular forum sites in your niche by running a Google search for 'your topic + forums'. For instance, continuing with the earlier weight loss example, you can see that there is no shortage of forums in this particular market.

Check the rules of the most popular forums, confirming whether you can use a signature file or not. If so, this is another highly targeted way of advertising your business as your signature file is a short two or three line description of what you do in which you are usually allowed to add an active hyperlink to your site.

Every time you add a post or start your own thread in this form, your signature file will be shown and read by other members who are already extremely interested in the topic of your product. Thus, adding a signature file in this way is a highly effective strategy for sending super-targeted prospects to your site very quickly.

Another thing that you can do is visit targeted blogs in your market sector to leave comments on them. If you make sure that these comments are both valid and valuable, you are adding fresh new content to the blog so it is almost certain that the owner will publish your comment.

Short on Cash?

Use Google blog search to find niche targeted blogs in your sector and set aside some time every day to investigate and comment on blogs as appropriate.

Another thing that you should always do is make sure that you post information to the major social bookmarking sites every time you add content either to your own site or to a site like YouTube.

Use a resource like Social Poster or Social Marker to speed up the submission process, making sure that every time you submit information, you use two or three of your main keyword phrases as tags.

However, although it might be very tempting to do so, do not submit information about every piece of content you publish to every one of the social bookmarking sites because that begins to look like spam. Instead, choose half a dozen social sites at random every time you want to make a submission and change the sites that you are submitting to every time you do so.

One thing about this particular strategy is that what you have just created is essentially a fully-fledged online business.

Consequently, whilst you can use this particular tactic for generating cash fairly quickly, it is also highly effective for generating money over the longer term as well.

For this reason, you might also use longer term traffic generation tactics such as article marketing to bring targeted visitors in relatively slowly, knowing that the traffic flow will continue for months or even years into the future.

Chapter 6- Write or Teach for Your Love of Money

Do you love writing? Have you always dreamed of writing a bestseller novel? Well, most successful novelists also had a day job. Here's a day job that can keep you in the writing field that you love so much and also pay you a decent salary, so that you can still have time left over for your blockbuster novel!

Anyone with a good grasp of the English language can write a few paragraphs of original content. It is even easier to just read a given article and rewrite it. And that is pretty much the job description for one of the most lucrative jobs on the Internet today.

With thousands of new websites being set up every hour, webmasters are in constant need of new content for their webpages. Sometimes a number of websites are developed by spinning the same content into several articles. Most buyers of articles pay between one to two dollars for rewriting an article of

Short on Cash?

300- 500 words. This task can be done in fifteen to thirty minutes depending on your language skills and typing speed.

It is important to write original content – say it all in your own words – as most buyers check for duplication by using copy-detection software like Copyscape and Plagium. If you just cut and paste from some other websites, that will show up on Copyscape and you will lose your assignment and get negative reviews from the buyer.

Proofread your article thoroughly before submitting it, using Spellcheck if you use Word. Even if you aren't familiar with a topic like say acne or money management or health topics, some time spent browsing relevant websites can give you enough information to write a 500 word article.

That's the charm of freelance writing online. Your general knowledge improves vastly with the articles you research and write every day. That will surely help your creative writing too, and pave the way for that blockbuster novel someday!

Write eBooks

When the Internet first became popular, it was looked upon mostly as a portal for information and communication. The information part was actually very poignant, because people didn't have such a splendid method of finding what they wanted whenever they wanted. This impression of the Internet persists even today. Even today, the Internet is an information superhighway and people with an astute mind are making the most of it in various ways.

One of the most significant ways is through creating and selling eBooks. EBooks, or electronic books, are books filled with information on one particular subject. It covers a part of that subject, and is generally (but not always) a self-help guide. Well, those are the ones that make the most money and hence are the most popular, anyway.

The concept is simple. Take something that people are searching for information on, and create an eBook about it. Write in a simple, crisp manner in a language that even a layperson can understand. When you have the eBook ready, promote it over the Internet. There are various ways to do that – make a webpage, create a sales page, advertise through affiliates, promote the eBook on social networking websites, etc. The more you make your eBook popular, the more people will want to have it.

Now, there are two ways in which you can make money out of your eBooks. You could either sell them directly for money, or you could use them to sell a bigger product. When you do the latter, you may not even charge for your eBook. The concept of giving away is very much real on the Internet, and it does attract a lot of interested people to buy bigger products.

So, what can you write the eBook on? Think about anything you know that you think people might like to know about. It could be about anything – about how to clean glass windows the right way or about how to look for mortgage providers for your new nest. The idea is to teach, and to make money out of that teaching.

Short on Cash?
Teaching Online Could Make You Rich

One of the most enjoyable ways to earn money online is by selling some skill that you are good at.

Can you teach a language or show how to fix a clogged drain? Just pick up a digital camera and shoot yourself doing your thing. Then upload it onto YouTube. Circulate the link to everyone you know and also place it on related forums. Then build a simple specialized website with more such learning videos. Arrange to give access only to viewers who pay a small fee via credit card or PayPal. Place the link to this website on your free YouTube videos.

As your videos gain thousands of hits, your website will be visited by more subscribers and you can begin to earn money. You can also create eBooks on your particular subject and sell them on that website.

Place a lot of related links to similar websites that may be useful to your members. You may think this may take viewers away from your webpage. But subscribers appreciate this kind of honesty and help and they will keep coming back to you.

This way you keep doing what you love, and the world pays you for it. Setting up a webpage or blog free of cost (Blogger.com), monitoring traffic (Sitemeter.com) and creating eBooks (eBook Pro) are easily done by using any of the hundreds of tools available on the Internet.

By working at home, you have the advantage of using your home premises, utilities and fixtures with no extra shop costs. You can set up a small studio to teach an art skill like sculpting or making candles or even simple handmade cards. There are thousands of YouTube videos teaching music and dance.

Find your niche and go for it. It will take a little time to build up your business, but if you do something special, it will spread virally via YouTube and you can then capitalize on your success.

Interview an Expert in Your Niche

The fastest way of creating your own product that you can then start selling is by interviewing experts in your niche market.

This is in fact probably the easiest and quickest way of creating your own product from scratch and because most people will allow you to interview them without asking for an upfront fee, it is also an extremely cheap way of doing the job as well.

Of course, you will have to give your expert something in return for their time and effort, but more often than not, you can do this by coming to some arrangement about giving them a percentage of the money generated by product sales.

As an example, you may split the revenue generated by selling the interview series with them, and/or you might include a One-Time Offer (OTO) from which they receive a split as well. As the name implies, the idea behind the One-Time Offer is that just before or immediately after the customer has completed their initial product purchase, they are presented with an offer for a product which they are only ever going to see once (hence the name).

Whenever you sell your own product, whether it is an e-book or an interview series with an expert, you must always include a backend sale (the 'would you like fries with that?' approach), and it is generally more effective to do so as an OTO.

Another thing to understand is that whilst the more well-known your interviewee is, the more sales you're likely to generate, it is

Short on Cash?

not absolutely essential that you manage to land an interview with a household name the very first time you do this. In fact, it is pretty unlikely that you will be to do so without any provable track record of creating a product of this type before, so you might have to set your sights a little lower the very first time you do this.

However, this will not kill your sales because it is up to you to emphasize and (if possible) magnify the expert status of your interviewee. After all, as long as they have something of value to teach or tell anyone who buys the interview series you create, your customer is getting the value for which they are paying.

The easiest and cheapest way of interviewing your expert is to interview them on the 'telephone' using a service like Skype or something similar. Use appropriate free software to record the conversation as an MP3 file, and you have your interview in the bag without moving from the comfort of home.

Now, you can either make the interview series available as a digital download only, or you can enhance the value of the service you are offering (thereby allowing you to charge more money for your product) by physically delivering a hard copy on CD or DVD of the interview directly to your customer's door. To do this, pay Kunaki$1.75 to produce each copy for you including a case, labels etc.:

Do this and you immediately enhance the value of the offer you making on your site, which will enable you to charge $27 for your interview product, rather than $17.

The final question therefore has to be, where do you find suitable interviewees who have sufficient knowledge and experience in your market niche to be able to provide value when interviewed? The simple answer is, go back to the forums that you were frequenting earlier because no matter what niche you're working in, you will usually find the best-known experts frequenting the most popular and active forum sites.

As a simple example, if you were looking for an internet marketing expert or online business guru, your first port of call would undoubtedly be the Warrior Forum. I am not personally aware of anyone who I would seriously consider to be an online marketing expert who is not a member of this particular forum. From my experience of other niches, this seems to be a fairly common characteristic of the best-known forums in all markets.

If you already know who the best-known experts in your market sector are, then you can probably search the popular forums to find whether a particular individual is a member by name.

As a general rule, I have found that because these experts often use their name as a recognizable brand, most will use their ordinary names when they join forums of this type. Hence, a simple search may find the person you're looking for.

If on the other hand you are not already familiar with the best-known people in your market sector, it is often fairly easy to find these people by watching what is going on in your favorite forum site.

One dead-giveaway is when someone starts a new thread or post that is not particularly contentious (and not even especially interesting in many examples) that all of a sudden seems to become incredibly popular. Check a few of the posts that have been added to a thread like this and you will often find that many of them are nothing more than 'Way to go, Bob' or 'Well said, John' type comments.

Short on Cash?
This indicates that none of these posters has anything particularly valuable to add to this thread but they want to be seen because they are trying to be associated with the individual who started the thread in the first place. This is always a strong indicator of someone who is highly respected and well known in the business, so take note of their name and keep an eye on their activity for a short while to confirm your initial suspicion that they are indeed regarded as an expert in your market.

Another thing that can help point you in the direction of recognized experts is the number of posts that they have added to the forum which you are investigating. If someone is capable of adding thousands of posts to any individual form, it suggests that they have a great deal of knowledge and probably experience as well, so they are probably the kind of person you want to interview.

CHAPTER 7- YOU HAVE POTENTIAL INCOME WITH AFFILIATE MARKETING

Affiliate marketing is a very popular concept on the Internet. Basically, it is a way in which you promote someone else's product on your webpage or blog and earn money for driving people to the advertiser's website. These people that you send are known as traffic. The payment is usually through a PPC method (not unlike Google AdSense). You are paid per click that you generate on the advertiser's website link. However, there are other payment models as well, such as PPS (where you are paid per sale) and PPL (where you are paid per lead).

Now, here is a method that can help you earn money even as you sleep. Once you set up the ad and put your promotional campaigns in place, people will automatically keep getting directed to the

Short on Cash?

advertiser's website, which means you automatically start getting money. This kind of money, which comes in without doing anything constantly, is known as residual income or passive income.

Your basic efforts here are at publicizing your own website or blog so that the affiliate links on them become visible and more people click on them. Your income is directly proportionate to the number of people that you manage to send. You could popularize your website through several other instant cash strategies mentioned here, such as article writing and submission, blogging, etc.

One of the main reasons why affiliate marketing is popular today is because the payment is really long-term. The money just keeps coming if you have done things rightly. Unlike other methods, the payment here comes in, regardless of the amount of effort you put in. A few months of careful planning and implementing can bring in thousands of dollars a month into your coffers. However, this is an instant cash method as well, because the money will start coming almost instantly, usually within the first week itself.

Chapter 8 - Domain Flipping and Website Spinning

Buying and selling domain names can be an exceptionally lucrative venture to get into, however if you are starting off with very little cash flow, it's always best to purchase lower cost domains and generate small profits as you work your way up to larger flips.

I have sold hundreds of domain names that I secured from marketplaces like EBay and resold on marketplaces like NamePros.com or DNForum.com.

While the marketplaces where domain sales are most lucrative will change from that of website flipping, the game remains the same with your focus being on locating and purchasing low cost domains and flipping them for a higher price.

Short on Cash?

One of the great aspects of domain flipping is that the efforts required are minimal. No longer must you locate or integrate content, tweak website pages, outsource tasks, or transfer websites.

All you need to do is find memorable, appealing domain names in niche markets and sell them to buyers, eager to create their own website on this domain.

Furthermore, the risks are quite low as are the investment costs, and once you have set up your system so that you are generating daily profits, it will require no more than one hour a day to keep the cash flow going.

Many of my partners, students and friends are earning $500 - $2,500 per week from flipping low cost domain names, while others have gone to secure high value domain names that are generating them revenue even before they are resold.

It's not a difficult business to get into, if you follow my simple guide to buying and selling domain names.

To start, you will want to create accounts at places, where you can both buy and sell domain names.

How to Choose Domains that Sell

When it comes to finding the best domain names, the easiest route to take is in exploring the expired domain listings.

With expired domain names, it simply means that they have previously been registered and left to expire. These are far more appealing to buyers due to the fact that they are considered 'aged', despite the fact that they have expired and are no longer active domains.

Download lists of expired domain names each day, and run them through a filtering script. What this script will do is enable you to sort through the listings of domains by extension, as well as weed through domains that have numbers or hyphens. It's quite flexible in how you can set it up to filter through these lists for you, hands free. Best of all, it can handle very large text based lists.

When it comes to purchasing domain names for resale, you want to stick with the top level extension, the dot com, and avoid any domains with numbers, or other characters.

You will also want to focus on searching for expired domain names that are as short as possible, and with utilities such as the one available at alouwebdesign.ca, you are able to search through your lists by setting a maximum and minimum length, meaning that you can sort through the domains so that only ones that are shorter will appear.

Personally, I set the maximum length to 20 characters and of course, the minimum to zero, so that it includes the shortest domain names on my expired lists.

You will also need to enter in specific keywords, these are words that when contained within any of the expired domains, will be included in the results page after you have entered in your list and filtered through the results.

Creating a keyword swipe file is an ongoing job, and one that you should concentrate a lot of effort on, as the more prime keywords you enter into the software, the better your chances of finding true gems.

Short on Cash?

This comes down to the niche markets you cater to, and you should take a bit of time to start creating a list of keywords in a text file that you can copy and paste into the software.

Apart from targeted keywords, you should also consider thinking outside the box a bit, by drumming up a list of memorable keywords that when added to a domain can be used for branding purposes.

I've sold countless domain names contrived of two keywords that really made no sense together but because of the sound, the appeal and the "brandability" factor, they were gobbled up quickly.

Think about some of the Internet's most popular websites like Twitter.com, Facebook.com or FeedBurner.com whose domains are off the beaten path but definitely memorable, which is one of the best important elements of domain names profitability.

Take some time to get familiar with both the expired domain websites as well as the software available to help you manage the lists and weed through potential gems.

Once you have sorted through your lists, it's time to run the remaining domains through a bulk domain registration tool, to determine what domains are still available, as others downloading these lists may have scooped up a few already.

The only problem with expired domain listings are that if you don't move quickly, a lot of the better domain names will be snatched up as these lists tend to get distributed all over the Internet rather quickly.

Another obstacle when browsing through expired domain lists is the fact that often times domain registrars will snag any domains that have existing traffic.

This means that some of the domain names on the lists will not become available after they have expired, but instead, held by the domain registrars for a period of 5-7 days before potentially being dropped and made available again.

The best way to address this is to go over each lists (and as many different lists as you can), taking notes of any domain names that are appealing.

Write them down in a text file and every day; take a few minutes to check whether the domains have become available to the public.

Before you do this however, you should know that there are many domain registrars online that will literally steal your domain research.

What this means is that when you type the domain name into your browser to see if it's available, or if you visit a domain registrar's website and enter in a domain to see its status, these companies analyze this data and may snap up a domain you are considering.

This has been happening for many years and has recently caused quite a stir amongst the domain community when some well-known registrars were caught doing this.

Hitting the Gold Mine with Aged Domains

Domains that have been registered and never dropped are called "Aged Domains".

Short on Cash?

These domains typically sell for more than a new one does because it has been around for a while, it's usually out of the Google Sandbox and for those who are looking for aged domains, it can help them develop an existence online, a history, or credibility in their niche markets simply because if the domain has been around for years, it appears that they have as well.

Aged domains can also be found on forums like DNForum.com and simply by typing in the keywords "Aged Domains" into the search bar you can easily locate domain auctions that include these older domain names.

I have purchased dozens of domain names for $40 or less that were anywhere from 5 – 10 years old. Just based on the age alone I was able to flip these domain names for over 5x what I paid.

For instance, one domain name I purchased was never used, meaning it had never featured a website on it; it just sat parked in the users account for over six years.

I purchased the domain for only $30.00 and because of its age, I was able to flip it for $379.00. That's quite a boost in profit from a domain I paid so little for.

While there is no exact science as to what type of domain names will ultimately be worth the most, apart from the obvious short and memorable domain names, there are a few things to keep in mind:

1)   Development Potential

When you analyze the available domains in your list, consider what each domain name could represent and be used for when creating a website presence.

An example of which is whether the domain name is one that could represent a product title, or better served as a personal portfolio, a social community, a directory or perhaps a forum.

While the purpose of the domain name will unlikely match your ideas when it is sold, by thinking of a clear purpose for each domain name will not only help you make sound choices during the selection process, but can also be included in the domain auction, as a way of passing on the ideas to prospective buyers who are considering purchase.

2) Length

It cannot be said enough, that the length of a domain name, apart from the odd occurrence where you locate a lengthy domain name that still carries with it, a memorable element, most of the domain names you purchase should be relatively short, basically consisting of two words.

3) Trademark Issues

Avoid registering any domain names that could infringe upon the trademark of existing companies, whether or not you believe that the company will take action or not should not be considered.

The last thing you want is to purchase a domain name that is unable to be sold due to buyers being cautious or concerned of building a website on a domain that ends up being seized by a company wishing to protect their identity.

Short on Cash?

4)	Relevant / Popular Keywords

Does the domain name contain popular keywords that are used by those seeking out more information in search engines? If so, your domain name just increased its value instantly.

5) Existing Traffic

If you are purchasing aged or recently expired domains, you will want to determine whether there is existing traffic to the website or not. If there is, its value will increase immensely.

Organic, natural traffic sent directly from search engines is the best kind, however back links from other websites are also very important to potential buyers.

Selling Domain Names

It's time to set up your domain names on eBay!

Before we do this however, there are a couple of important things to take into consideration:

1) If you are new to eBay, you should take some time to read their website and get to know how their auctions work, as well as the applicable fees and listing options.

2) You can lose a lot of money buying into the bells & whistles so avoid purchasing any add-ons when you list your domain names. You do not need a featured listing, a highlighted auction title, or any of that silly stuff.

3) Your feedback rating is very important with anything you sell on eBay, whether it's domain names or children's toys. People judge

you based on the feedback you have received so if you have any negative feedback, I would suggest creating a new eBay account.

If you are brand new to eBay, there is little you can do to generate positive feedback quickly, other than to ensure that you follow through with your auctions, keep open communication with your buyers and be prompt when pushing your domain names after they have been purchased. Never make them wait more than 24 hours for their domain.

4) Open a PayPal account; it's almost required in order to sell on eBay these days. People prefer PayPal and it just makes things a lot easier.

You can open and verify a PayPal account within a couple of days, so do your best to set this up prior to listing your auctions.

5) Choose a relevant eBay username. Don't try to be trendy and pick some crazy sounding username, choose one specifically for domain and/or site flipping. Something like DomainExperts or DomainTrends would be just fine. If you end up not liking what you chose you can change it every 30 days.

When you list your auctions on eBay, you should start them all off at $.99. Do not place a reserve on these auctions, and do not add any restrictions or limitations of any kind.

Just set them up individually, and list them at $.99 each to start.

For beginners the idea of paying $8 for a domain name and listing it at $.9 is nerve wracking however with a lower start-up price, you will entice more bidders to participate and your auction will boost up in price quickly.

Short on Cash?
Once people become attached to the domain, they will create a bidding war against any other user who tries to take it away from them and you will see your auction soar as it gets closer to the end of the time, so don't be too nervous about losing money.

Note: If you have paid more than the basic registration of a domain name, meaning that you have purchased a domain name for more than $7-9, depending on what you paid for the domain you may want to start the auction off on a higher amount, just be aware that the lower the startup bid, the more activity it will receive.

By not listing a reserve fee you will also be able to list your domains on eBay at a lower cost, as eBay charges sellers a fee for including a reserve price. You should also pay attention to eBay listing sales, which occur from time to time and feature reduced fee auctions. Whenever there is a sale, list as many domains as you can to save yourself a bundle in listing fees.

I also do not recommend that you feature a BIN (Buy It Now) price either, as you may end up short-changing yourself if you list the BIN at a lower price than others are willing to pay. Let the auction determine its own price and run its course.

When selling your domain names on eBay, always choose a relevant category.

Also be sure to include a direct headline to your auction listing, which describes the domain name you are featuring. Include the domain name in full within your auction title.

And most importantly, ALWAYS include a domain "idea", something that can provoke thought and get potential buyers to consider the various options that are available to them when using the domain name:

Edward Clark

Always include the domain registrar, the age (unless it's brand new than do not include it), and utilize the free option to include a gallery picture just because research has shown that auctions showcasing a photo of any kind will receive more attention.

When creating the body text of your listing, you want to provide as many ideas for possible use as you can, as well as giving them as much information relating to the auction as possible such as:

Payments Accepted and your terms (Payment is due within two days of auction, etc.)

Transfer Time – How quickly you can push the domain over after payment is received, (I always include "Transfer within 24 Hours of Payment Receipt")

And a link to any other domain auctions that you currently have going. This is very important and it's a great way to inter-link your auctions and encourage multiple purchases from your buyers since they can purchase as many as they like and pay all at once v' the eBay checkout system.

The link to your other auctions is available under "S Other Items". Just right click and choose "Copy Link" and a new link in your listing that links to one another.

This takes time but it's definitely worthwhile!

Also be sure to include how long the domain ed for, so buyers can determine how soon they will be renew it.

There are a lot of buyers who will not p' main name that is due to expire within two mo' have just

Short on Cash?

registered the domain name, then be sure to emphasize the fact that it is only expiring in a year's time.

When listing your auction you can choose the time frame in which it will remain active. I typically choose the 7 or 10 day auction plan.

Be sure that you are available on the day that your auction ends and that you answer any questions that you receive during the course of your auction (and you can expect a handful).

Also be sure to include contact information. When someone purchases a domain from you, depending on the registrar that you use, you may be required to obtain specific information from your buyer in order to push the domain into their account.

Spinning Websites

This is an instant cash method that many people like. It makes good money doesn't need a terrible lot of effort and is creative as well. However, you need to have a modicum of technical knowledge to begin with. Again, that shouldn't deter you. Even if you don't have the technical knowledge, you can still hire someone to do things that aren't comfortable with.

So, is website spinning actually? This is a method in which people build websites and then sell them over for a profit. The basis of making the website is to be able to sell it later. The will be good if the website is good.

Here are things that website spinners keep in mind.

→ The right domain names. In fact, a lot of their talent lies here. Make sure that the domain names are good SEO and that have recall value as well.

→ They build short websites. The websites aren't kept too large because then it becomes difficult to flip them. A usual website that is designed for flipping contains no more than 10 pages.

→ The websites are kept rich in content. The content is meant to educate. Once again, the content is high SEO, containing a lot of keywords that people commonly search for.

→ The design and the overall look of the website are kept quite basic. The reason for that is to enable the buyer to tweak the website according to their desires.

The proceeds of the sale depend on how good the website is. The least you could expect for a website of 10 pages is $50, which is not bad for starters. If your website already has some popularity on Google, you could sell it for much higher.

The selling is done on forums. A good place to sell is the Digital Point Forums.

ABOUT THE AUTHOR

Edward Clark is an internet marketing expert who has earned millions without leaving the comforts of his home. He provides webinars and offers one-on-one consultations to help businesses thrive and succeed in their chosen niche markets.

www.ingramcontent.com/pod-product-compliance
Lightning Source LLC
Chambersburg PA
CBHW051254290125
21063CB00018BA/210